The Life and Death of
Rochester Sneath

The Life and Death of
Rochester Sneath

A Youthful Frivolity

Humphry Berkeley
Nicolas Bentley drew the pictures

DAVIS POYNTER LONDON [dp]

First published in 1974 by Davis-Poynter Limited
20 Garrick Street London WC2E 9BJ
Second impression 1975

Copyright © 1974 by Humphry Berkeley
Illustrations copyright © 1974 by Nicolas Bentley

ISBN 0 7067 0150 X

Text layout by Mike Jarvis

Printed in Great Britain by
Bristol Typesetting, Barton Manor, Bristol

To Robin Bidwell, for his help

Contents

Introduction

Twenty-six years ago, when I was an undergraduate at Cambridge, I invented a public school. It was called Selhurst and its headmaster bore the name of H. Rochester Sneath.

This fictitious school was intended to be a minor but respectable school in what one might term the third league, as public schools go. Mr Rochester Sneath was an unusual, not to say eccentric, headmaster and if the readers of this book trace a resemblance between him and Dr Fagan of Evelyn Waugh's *Decline and Fall* they would not be altogether wrong, since I had recently read this masterpiece and still believe it to be, of its kind, the best book that Evelyn Waugh ever wrote.

I was anxious that the school should possess a plausible name. For several months I would hold conversations with those of my fellow undergraduates who were comparative strangers to me. Invariably I would steer, or sometimes even wrench, the conversation to the point where I was asked the name of the school at which I had been educated. I did not answer with firm conviction that I had been to Eton or Rugby. Instead I gave a more diffident reply: 'Well as a matter of fact I was at a school called Selhurst.' This invariably produced on the face of my questioner a blank and slightly puzzled look. 'Haven't you heard of Selhurst?' I would ask, in the tone of an aggrieved party at law. ' Of course, I've heard of it my dear fellow,' would come the reply. 'Let's see, where exactly is it?' After a dozen or so conversational gambits of this nature I knew that I had chosen the perfect name. Nobody if challenged would admit that they had not heard of Selhurst.

I then had some letter headings printed headed: 'SELHURST SCHOOL NEAR PETWORTH SUSSEX, FROM THE HEADMASTER, H. ROCHESTER SNEATH.' At the total expense of fifteen shillings and an arrangement with the Post Office that they would forward any letter addressed to Selhurst to some lodgings of a friend of mine in Cambridge, I was able to embark on a series of correspondences with other headmasters and public figures.

This was the only practical joke that I have played in my life. The frivolity of a boy of twenty-one would be unpardonable in a man of forty-seven. At the time of discovery of the hoax, I was barred from visiting my college for two years. The last time that I visited Pembroke College, Cambridge I dined on the High Table and afterwards was persuaded by the Senior Fellow to relate the tale of Selhurst and Rochester Sneath to an audience of dons.

I have shown the letters included in this book to many personal friends in the intervening period, all of whom have said that they should be made available to a wider audience. None of the letters were intended to be malicious or to wound at the time but I decided that I would wait for twenty-five years before they could be published. All are genuine. Full marks must go to the then Headmaster of Winchester, Walter Oakshot, and the then Headmaster of Wimbledon College, The Rev John Sinnott SJ, who were the only two people to see through the hoax. I am grateful to Robin Bidwell, an undergraduate contemporary, for his help.

I hope that my reputation is such that I will no longer be compared with the frivolous boy of twenty-five years ago. In self defence I must say that I gained an honourable degree and became President of the Union and Chairman of the Cambridge University Conservative Association, while I was an undergraduate. So my university days, the happiest in my life, were not wasted.

I have called this book *The Life and Death of Rochester Sneath*, and I have given it the sub-title 'A Youthful Frivolity', which it was and is.

Humphry Berkeley, 1974

To the Headmaster of Selhurst School

Post Office
Petworth
Sussex

PO Ref 1576/326
March 25th, 1948

Dear Sir,

With reference to your letter of the 23rd instant, the redirection
of correspondence addressed to you at Selhurst School, Petworth,
has been noted for attention.

As, however the address 'Selhurst School' is not known in this
district perhaps you will be good enough to inform me of the
exact location of the School.

Yours faithfully,
F. A. Dean
Head Postmaster (Acting)

Post Office
Petworth
Sussex

April 14th, 1948

Dear Sir,

With further reference to your request for the redirection of
correspondence addressed to Selhurst School Near Petworth I have
to indicate that as detailed on page 55 of the Post Office Guide
the Post Office cannot undertake to effect this service when
redirection can be carried out at the place of address.

Your letter of the 27th ultimo suggests that the house is at
present occupied and I shall therefore be glad if its location is
furnished and arrangements made with the occupier to redirect
any correspondence addressed to yourself coming to hand.

The service at present performed by the Post Office will cease
after the 19th instant.

Yours faithfully,
J. A. Richardson
Head Postmaster

To the Master of Marlborough College

Selhurst School
Near Petworth
Sussex

March 15th, 1948

Dear Master,

As you are probably aware this summer sees the 300th anniversary of the foundation of Selhurst. In view of our connection with Royalty and the fact that at the beginning we numbered among our pupils the nephew of a Balkan Monarch, I am most anxious to have the honour of entertaining Their Majesties if this is at all feasible.

Perhaps you would be kind enough to let me know how you managed to engineer a visit recently from the King and Queen.

Perhaps you would also give me any tips which you may have learned from your visit as to how Royalty should be treated since Selhurst would certainly wish the scale of its hospitality to be second to none.

With kind regards and all good wishes.

Yours sincerely,
H. Rochester Sneath
Headmaster

The College
Marlborough
Wilts

March 19th, 1948

Dear Mr Sneath,

I have your letter of March 15th. I did nothing whatever to engineer the recent Royal visit, I merely received a communication from the King's Private Secretary saying that the King and Queen could visit the school on March 12th if that day would be convenient.

No doubt the fact that the King's Private Secretary, the Lord Chancellor and the Archbishop of Canterbury are all Old Marlburians had something to do with the matter.

I simply made arrangements for the day when I knew that the King and Queen would come.

I am in no position to help you in your request.

Yours truly,
F. M. Heywood
Master

Selhurst School
Near Petworth
Sussex

March 26, 1948

Dear Heywood,

I am writing you this letter in the strictest confidence. I understand from a Mr Robert Agincourt who was Senior French Master at Selhurst, for one term two years ago, that he is applying for a post on the staff of Marlborough College.

He has asked me if I could give him a testimonial to present to you and I told him that by no stretching of veracity was I able to do this. You will understand that nothing that I have to say about Mr Agincourt is actuated by any personal malice but I feel it my duty to inform you of the impression that he gave while he was at Selhurst.

During his brief stay no less than five boys were removed from the school as a result of his influence, and three of the Matrons had nervous breakdowns. The pictures on the walls of his rooms made a visiting Bishop shudder and would certainly rule out another Royal visit. His practices were described by the Chairman of the County Hospital as 'Hunnish'. The prominent wart on his nose was wittily described as 'the blot on the twentieth century' by a visiting conjuror.

As you can not fail to have noticed, his personal appearance is against him, and, after one memorable Carol Service, a titled Lady who was sitting next to him collapsed in a heap. He was once observed climbing a tree in the School Grounds naked at night and on another occasion he threw a flower pot at the wife of the Chairman of the Board of Governors.

Should you wish any further information, I should be glad to furnish it for I could not wish another Headmaster to undergo the purgatory that I suffered that term.

I am staying for some days with my sister Mrs Harvey-Kelly at Castle Brae, Chesterton, Cambridge and I would be grateful if you would reply to this address.

Yours sincerely,
H. Rochester Sneath
Headmaster

The College
Marlborough
Wilts

March 28th, 1948

Dear Mr Sneath,
The man whom you have mentioned has not made any approach to me and I require no further information about him.

Yours truly,
F. M. Heywood
Master

Selhurst School
Near Petworth
Sussex

April 2nd, 1948

My dear Heywood,

I am sorry to trouble you yet again but I thought it right to inform you that Mr Agincourt has abandoned the idea of an academic career and has now become a waiter in a Greek restaurant in Soho.

Incidentally, I dined with the Lord Chancellor last night and he spoke of you to me in the highest possible terms.

There are just two thing that you can do for me. In the first place I am anxious to engage a private detective and would be grateful if you could give me the name of the man you normally use. Could you also recommend a competent nursery maid?

With kind regards.

Yours ever,
H. Rochester Sneath
Headmaster

The College
Marlborough
Wilts

April 4th, 1948

Dear Mr Sneath,

I cannot imagine why you should suppose that I employ a private detective, and I am not an agency for domestic servants.

I really must ask you not to bother me with this kind of thing.

Yours truly,
F. M. Heywood
Master

Mr Robert Agincourt

To Mr George Bernard Shaw

Selhurst School
Near Petworth
Sussex

Dear Mr Bernard Shaw,
    In view of the long-standing connection between your late wife's family and Selhurst School I am emboldened to invite you to be present at the tricentenary celebrations of the foundation of the School, which will be taking place during the weekend of the 19–20th June, honoured by the presence of the Minister of Education, Mr George Tomlinson. I venture to hope that you might be willing to address a few words to our boys, and, should you accept, I will be glad if you would take as your text 'A Clarion Call to Youth'. Incidentally you may remember meeting me in Dublin some years ago.

Yours sincerely,
H. Rochester Sneath
Headmaster

> Mr Bernard Shaw has long since been obliged by advancing years to retire from his committees and his personal activities on the platform. He therefore begs secretaries of societies to strike his name from their lists of available speakers. Mr Shaw does not open exhibitions or bazaars, take the chair, speak at public dinners, give his name as vice-president or patron, make appeals for money on behalf of hospitals or 'good causes' (however deserving), nor do any ceremonial public work. Neither can he take part in new movements nor contribute to the first numbers of new magazines. He begs his correspondents to excuse him accordingly.

Never heard of any such connection. Too old ($91\frac{3}{4}$) anyhow.

G. B. S.

Ayot Saint Lawrence
Welwyn, Herts
29/3/1948

To Sir William Reid Dick

Selhurst School
Near Petworth
Sussex

April 22nd, 1948

Dear Sir William Reid Dick,

As you may perhaps be aware, Selhurst is this year to celebrate the third centenary of its foundation. A committee has been formed, and it has been decided that a statue should be erected in the forecourt. I have been asked to enquire if you would undertake the work, for it is the opinion of the Committee that none but the best will do for Selhurst. The details of size and material could be settled at a later date. Unfortunately no authentic portrait exists of our founder, the Puritan leader Ebenezer Okeshot, although I understand that there was one by Vandyck that was believed to be of him. I have been unable to trace it and have been told, indeed, that it was in Rotterdam and destroyed at the time of the 'blitz'. Unless a portrait appears in time, the Committee has decided that a figure in Puritan dress should be erected. I am flattered to say that they wish the face and figure to be modelled from my own. I do not know whether this would be possible, but you could arrange that with the Committee, should you accept the commission.

I shall be staying for a few days with my sister Mrs Harvey-Kelly at Castle Brae, Chesterton, Cambridge and it would save time and trouble if you would reply there.

Yours sincerely,
H. Rochester Sneath
Headmaster

Sixteen Maida Vale
W 9

April 24th, 1948

Dear Mr Rochester Sneath,

    I am interested in the proposed statue for Selhurst School and I would like, if possible, to have some details of the founder, Ebenezer Okeshot. I should also like to see the site so as to determine the scale of the statue.

Yours sincerely,
W. Reid Dick

A transitory phase

To the Headmaster of Rugby

Selhurst School
Near Petworth
Sussex

April 24th, 1948

Dear fforde,

Please forgive my having taken so long in writing to congratulate you upon your appointment at Rugby. Unfortunately, dear boy, I have been ill and unable to attend to correspondence for three months, but as an old friend of your good father's (I used to fag for him at School), I felt that he would wish me to give you some advice. The running of a School is a complex business. You will find, as I did when I came here as a young Headmaster nearly thirty-five years ago, that there are many Senior Masters who must be treated with tact. My first term here my Senior Housemaster committed suicide after eloping with the matron, but I hope that you will be spared that. On the other hand, you are bound to find a certain amount of resentment, especially among the older Masters, and, from my long experience, I would counsel you to treat them with deference although it may be only too clear that they do not deserve it. Always remember that one staunch friend among his Staff is an invaluable asset to any Headmaster. But something more than this is needed, and this is tolerance. Remember that you are a man of the world, as indeed I was when I became Headmaster, and you cannot expect the same broad-mindedness from men whose mental stature is inevitably circumscribed by the narrowness of the school surroundings. Never forget that the School exists for the boys and not the boys for the School, and that a quiet chat over a glass of sherry with a miscreant will often effect more than an out-of-hand beating. Do not be taken in by the hysterical outcries against homosexuality which from time to time appear in the press. I have found that most homosexuality amongst schoolboys is harmless, and you can afford to ignore what is in most cases a purely transitory phase. Do not quote me as saying this, because although I believe it to be true, you cannot say that kind of thing to the parents. When you meet difficulties, as indeed you are bound to, do not hesitate to write to me for advice, which I will gladly give for your good father's sake.

I am spending the next fortnight with my sister Mrs Harvey-Kelly at Castle Brae, Chesterton, Cambridge, and would be glad to hear from you there.

Yours sincerely,
H. Rochester Sneath
Headmaster

Archers
Headley
Hants

May 1st, 1948

My dear Mr Sneath,

I must congratulate you, in turn, on your restoration to health : and thank you for writing me a letter so closely packed with good and servicable advice : tending, it seems to me, to show, on the whole and so far as my own experience of people in other walks of life has gone, that if Civil Servants and Solicitors can, as is probable, be described with a rough accuracy as human beings, the same is probably true of Schoolmasters.

But I wouldn't know : and, when in trouble, will accept, at its word, your kind offer of advice.

Yours sincerely,
Arthur fforde

To the Headmaster of Sherborne

Selhurst School
Near Petworth
Sussex

April 23rd, 1948

Dear Headmaster,

I am writing to you upon a very distressing topic. One of my boys who was going up to London in the train some days ago leant out of the window to watch the Sherborne School train pass. As he was standing with his head out of the window, his School cap was snatched from his head and taken away in the Sherborne train. That alone would be a matter of some gravity in these days of shortages and would concern all who are hostile to such lawless behaviour. He has since, however, received an anonymous letter from your School which said that they had seen the name written inside the cap, and that it was intended to put it on the head of the Guy to be burned next November. I am sure that an act which coupled wanton vandalism with a deliberate insult to another Public School will be prevented by you in any possible way. I should be grateful if you would be able to return the cap or to obtain compensation from the culprit at the earliest possible moment.

I shall be staying for a few days with my sister Mrs Harvey-Kelly at Castle Brae, Chesterton, Cambridge, and would be grateful if you would reply there.

Yours truly,
H. Rochester Sneath
Headmaster

The Headmaster
Sherborne School
Dorset

April 25th, 1948

Dear Headmaster,
    Thank you for your letter of April 23rd, which has given me very great concern. I should be grateful if you would send me the anonymous letter so that I may identify the writing when the boys come back. I shall catch the culprit right enough if I can have this. I shall not be able to do anything until the boys return of course, which is next Friday, but I should have the culprit by Monday morning. There is absolutely nothing to be said in my view in defence of such barbarous behaviour.
    I will let you know what transpires later on. Thank you for letting me know so promptly.

Yours truly,
A. R. Wallace

The Headmaster
Sherborne School
Dorset

May 4th, 1948

Dear Headmaster,
    I received a letter from you on April 23rd to which I replied on April 25th giving the address on your notepaper Selhurst School, Near Petworth, Sussex. I enclose a copy of my first letter, which has just been returned to me by the Post Office. I cannot understand it, and am therefore going to address this to your sister, Mrs Harvey-Kelly, and hope that she will kindly forward it to you.
    I repeat my apology for the behaviour of the Sherborne boy. I should be very grateful, and so would the Housemasters, if we could have the following information in order to trace the culprit :
    1. The date upon which the incident took place.
    2. The nearest station to the place of the incident.

3. Any description available of the boy who snatched the cap.
4. The actual letter sent from Sherborne which you mentioned in your letter. This is in itself a difficulty as none of the boys are here during the holidays.

If you will be good enough to supply these details it will help us considerably in narrowing down our enquiries.

Yours truly,
Alexander Wallace

To the Headmaster of Charterhouse

Selhurst School
Near Petworth
Sussex

March 15th, 1948

My dear Headmaster,

In view of our slight acquaintance on the football field many years ago, when, incidentally, you were responsible for breaking my collar-bone, I am venturing to write to you to ask you for your help in a matter of some delicacy. The nomination of Selhurst is to come before the Committee of the Headmasters' Conference at their next meeting. I feel that it would be a great help if I could secure the support of several prominent Headmasters, particularly those who know me personally, to assist our candidature. As you are probably aware Selhurst is a School of 275 boys and my staff, while consisting almost exclusively of graduates from Oxford and Cambridge, includes, a Doctor of Philosophy of Michigan University and a defeated Parliamentary candidate. Our Chaplain was considered for a Fellowship of his College and among our Old Alumni we are proud to include a coal miner, an income tax collector and a former Colonial Governor, not to mention a Canon of the Church of England.

The School has had to break up early as the result of a double epidemic and I am staying with my sister Mrs Harvey-Kelly at Castle Brae, Chesterton, Cambridge and would be glad if you would address your reply there.

Yours sincerely,
H. Rochester Sneath
Headmaster

The Headmaster
Charterhouse
Godalming

March 17th, 1948

Dear Mr Sneath,

Neither Mr Robert Birley, my predecessor, nor I plead guilty to having broken your collar-bone, and I think you must be confusing me with someone else in claiming our personal acquaintance.

There is a special committee of the Headmasters' Conference which deals with applications for membership, and I do not think that any personal representation is likely to affect its decision, which must rest upon certain established criteria. But I fear that recent applications may have to be turned down on the ground that the Conference has already reached the maximum of members allowed by its articles of association.

Yours very truly,
George Turner

To the Headmaster of Stowe

Selhurst School
Near Petworth
Sussex

April 22nd, 1948

Dear Headmaster,
    I understand that you have upon your staff a Master specially trained in the giving of instruction on the facts of sex. You will appreciate the delicacy of this matter and, I hope, forgive me thus for addressing you. Several lamentable happenings in recent weeks have brought home to me the complete ignorance of my boys upon this topic. After careful consideration, I have decided that a general lecture to the whole School, is the best. The writings upon the walls of the School lavatories made a visiting Bishop shudder and show how widespread is the trouble. The Chaplain has referred to the matter in his Lenten addresses, but feels that this is not enough. If, therefore, you could lend me the Master in question, I should be ever grateful. You will, of course, realise that the whole matter is in the strictest confidence.
    I am staying with my sister, Mrs Harvey-Kelly at Castle Brae, Chesterton, Cambridge, and it would save me some delay if you would kindly reply to that address.

Yours sincerely,
H. Rochester Sneath
Headmaster

Stowe
Buckingham

April 24th, 1948

Dear Sir,
    On behalf of the Headmaster (who is away on a short holiday) I write to acknowledge receipt of your letter of April 22nd, and in his absence I will endeavour to give you what help I can.
    The boys here receive instruction on the subject of your letter, but it is not given by one of our own masters. The talks are given by Dr Edward F. Griffith, a specialist in these matters, and his

The Chaplain's Lenten address

address is 25, Park Cresent, W 1. His talks to the various groups of boys are considered to be most helpful and instructive.

My few remarks are intended to save you some delay and I hope that they are of some use to you, but if you require further information I am sure Mr Roxburgh will gladly give it when he gets back to Stowe if you will kindly let him know.

Yours truly,
R. E. Lucas
Headmaster's Secretary

PRIVATE

Stowe
Buckingham

April 29th, 1948

Dear Mr Sneath,

I am sorry that I was away when your letter of April 22nd arrived here. Thinking it urgent my secretary replied to it but could only do so briefly. However, I believe that if I had written myself at the time I could not have said much more.

I will now only add that in my opinion a religious appeal on this question of sex is a mistake – except in so far as all religious training must cover *every* moral issue, including truth, kindness and courage as well as purity. The thing is best dealt with in as unemotional a manner as possible and without the element of mystery, hushed voices and vague allusions which so often make what a man says to a boy on these matters utterly unreal.

The first thing we do here is to see that no boy is left in ignorance of the physiological facts. For this purpose Dr Edward Griffiths comes from London and lectures to all the boys who are in their second term. He does this with slides and in a matter-of-fact and scientific manner. The next thing is to get Griffiths to lecture to all the boys who are in their fourth term on the difficulties of adolescence and on school problems. He lectures again to boys in their last term before they go out into the world. On all his visits he is available to have private discussions with any boy who wishes to see him.

In addition to this work done by Griffiths all the Housemasters are experienced in dealing with these problems with individual boys, and when need arises I sometimes deal with them myself— entirely on an individual basis. In doing so schoolmasters must, I think, have a real understanding of a boy's feelings and problems as well as a strong sense of what is right. But the guidance of adolescents can never be easy. It requires perpetual vigilance and a great deal of hard work.

If there is anything more that I can tell you of our practice here I hope that you will write to me again.

Yours sincerely,
J. F. Roxburgh

Selhurst School
Near Petworth
Sussex

April 29th, 1948

My dear Headmaster,

I am most grateful for the prompt reply of your Secretary and the useful information that he gives. I will contact Dr E. F. Griffith, but would be grateful if you would give me some preliminary information. In your experience would you think it better that the instruction should be given individually, in classes, or to the School as a whole? If given collectively do you find that it helps to have the Matrons and the Masters' wives present in the room, and would you advise special instruction for the School Maids?

Yours sincerely,
H. Rochester Sneath

Stowe
Buckingham

April 30th, 1948

Dear Mr Sneath,

Our letters have crossed. I am answering yours of the 29th only in order to say that I should strongly advise you *not* to include

Matrons, Masters' wives or any women in the room when Griffith is lecturing.

I am afraid I cannot help about the school maids, who are well looked after here by the Housekeeper and who never give any trouble.

I think that your other questions are answered in my letter of April 29th.

I am sorry, by the way, to see that Dr Griffith's name was by a typist's error spelt as Griffiths in my letter.

Yours sincerely,
J. F. Roxburgh

To the Headmaster of the Oratory

Selhurst School
Near Petworth
Sussex

April 22nd, 1948

Dear Headmaster,
   I understand that your School, like mine, had to undergo
the troubles of evacuation in the war. I thought, therefore, that
you might be interested to know that my Solicitors have discovered
that there is a loophole in the existing law that would enable us
to claim some quite substantial sums of money from the
Government. In these times when every class and interest seems
able to plunder the Exchequer, it seems a pity that really deserving
causes like the School should be left out in the cold. Also there
is the advantage that any sum gained could now be put into
something tangible as we have learned that a capital levy is likely
to become increasingly severe. If you would care to learn the details
we might fix up a meeting and, in all events, I must ask you to
keep the matter quiet. My Solicitors assure me that though no
charge in the Courts could result, the method might perhaps be
thought a trifle dishonest. However, it would be in a good cause,
and, surely for a Jesuit like yourself, that would be alright!

Yours very truly,
H. Rochester Sneath
Headmaster

From The Revd the Headmaster
The Oratory School
Woodcote
Nr Reading

April 24th, 1948

Dear Headmaster,
   Very many thanks for your letter of April 22nd. I am interested
in what you say of the possibility of making a claim on the
Government on account of evacuation of our premises during the
war.

I don't know whether it would apply in our case as we decided in the end to sell our former property at Caversham Park outright to the BBC. However, we lost nearly 100 boys by the move, and are now faced with the necessity of considerable extension to the property here, the estimate for which is hair-raising.

I have not the honour to belong to the Jesuits, but I shall none the less be interested to hear any further news on this subject which you may have to impart.

Yours sincerely,
G. A. Tomlinson

Selhurst School
Near Petworth
Sussex

April 29th, 1948

Dear Headmaster,

Thank you for your letter of April 24th. I have consulted my Solicitors again upon your problem and the fact that you have sold your former property without compulsion, unfortunately disqualifies you from any such claim. I regret having raised false hopes, but I was unaware of the full facts. I must also apologise for addressing you as a Jesuit, but I was under the impression that all Catholic Schools were owned by that Order.

Yours sincerely,
H. Rochester Sneath
Headmaster

To Sir Giles Gilbert Scott

Selhurst School
Near Petworth
Sussex

April 22nd, 1948

Dear Sir Gilbert Scott,

As you are perhaps aware, Selhurst is this term to celebrate the third centenary of its foundation. A Committee has been formed, and it has been decided to erect a new House to mark the occasion and to celebrate the rapid expansion of the School. It is, I am flattered to say, to be called Sneath House as one is already named after our Founder. The Committee has unanimously deputed me to ask if you would draw up a design for this House. You may perhaps be familiar with the façade of Selhurst, which Lord Palmerston said more nearly approximated to the vulgar idea of a Royal Palace than any country house he had seen in seventy years. Artists have of late somewhat neglected it, so we feel that its restoration, coupled with a design for an entirely new House will make a worthy object for our appeal. Experience will doubtless make you familiar with the sort of building a school like Selhurst will require. We do not wish for ostentation nor for luxury to enervate our pupils, yet youth is a tender plant and it cannot grow and develop in narrow and cramped surroundings. We would favour the sunlight let in upon our studies rather than the dark walls of a flanking building. We wish, naturally, that such things as laboratories where smells are habitual and explosions not unknown should be far from the quarters of the Masters and not too near to those of the boys. Above all, we wish for a building which will inspire clean and healthy thoughts and one in which it is easier to use the intellect than to slack. We do not wish to waste money on ornamentation which cannot be seen from the most important parts of the grounds where photographs are taken and parents are conducted. We do not wish to have profusion in the boys' rooms, which, from the very nature of things, are often unoccupied for long periods of the year. Finally, I should like to say that the superior dignity of the Masters to the boys, and of the Headmaster to the other Masters, should be properly safeguarded.

B

I am staying for some days with my sister, Mrs Harvey-Kelly at Castle Brae, Chesterton, Cambridge, and I should be grateful if you would reply there.

Yours sincerely
H. Rochester Sneath
Headmaster

Sir Giles Gilbert Scott, OM, RA
3 Field Court
Gray's Inn
London WC 1

April 26th, 1948

Dear Mr Sneath,

Selhurst School

Thank you for your letter of the 22nd inst., I am much gratified that you should have asked me to prepare a design for the new House. In other circumstances it would have given me the greatest pleasure to undertake this work, but the present situation is very difficult, as I am too heavily engaged with the Rebuilding of the House of Commons, the details of which are so complicated that they are taking up a very large proportion of my time. It would therefore be impossible for me to begin any work on the Selhurst scheme for the next twelve months.

I realise of course that this delay might by no means fit in with your arrangements, and if so I shall of course quite understand it.

I need not say that I am very sorry not to be able to send you a more favourable reply.

Yours sincerely
Giles Gilbert Scott

Protests from our Bishop

To Monsignor Ronald Knox

Selhurst School
Near Petworth
Sussex

April 24th, 1948

Dear Mgr Knox,

I hope that you will forgive this letter, for I feel that your advice would be of great value to me. My Chaplain and I have both read your translation of Holy Writ with interest and admiration, and we were considering their use in our own worship. I consider that this would be of great value to the Boys who so often find the standard versions so difficult for their young intelligences. In general we do not concentrate upon abstruse problems of theology but try to impress the ordinary rules of morality. We feel that The Public School Code means more than the philosophising of Hooker or of Thomas Aquinas. I should be grateful if you would inform me whether there have been any protests at its use by the ordinary laity for we would not wish to have a Jenny Geddes scene in our Chapel. You will understand that there is considerable opposition to anything that seems Romish but I hope that this will not be so regarded. Protests from our Bishop we can ignore for he has more than once threatened the Chaplain with excommunication, but remonstrances from parents are far more serious. I should be most grateful if you would tell me whether they are likely to occur.

I shall be staying for a few days with my sister, Mrs Harvey-Kelly at Castle Brae, Chesterton, Cambridge, and would be obliged if you would reply there.

Yours sincerely,
H. Rochester Sneath
Headmaster

The Manor House
Mells
Frome

April 30th, 1948

Dear Mr Rochester Sneath
    Thank you for your letter. As far as I know, all the barracking
over my version has come from my own co-religionists. Quakers,
Wesleyans, etc. use it freely, and Gordon Selwyn said in
Convocation that he turns it on in Winchester Cathedral when
St Paul is being extra obscure. So I don't think you'll find it
criticised as Romish.

Yours sincerely,
R. A. Knox

To the Rector of Beaumont College

Selhurst School
Near Petworth
Sussex

April 29th, 1948

Dear Rector of Beaumont,

I am writing to you upon a matter of some delicacy. As you may perhaps have read in one of the more prominent Psychic Journals, we at Selhurst are suffering from a troublesome ghost. In any old foundation such as ours, this is often to be expected, and this particular ghost is generally believed to be the spirit of a Matron who committed suicide at the beginning of the last century, after having been seduced by a Housemaster. I understand that Catholic priests alone are able to exorcise these ghosts with Holy Water, incense etc. I am told that Jesuits are particularly qualified for this owing to some degree they take, and that they would be more discreet than the local clergy. As this Spirit has already caused offence to a visiting Peeress, and, by appearing at dinner, has caused the wife of the Chairman of the Board of Governors to collapse in a heap, we are anxious to lay it as soon as possible, particularly as in a month's time we are to entertain the widow of an Ambassador. If you would consent to come, I should, of course, pay you the usual fee, and perhaps you would preach a sermon in our Chapel.

I shall be staying for about a fortnight with my sister Mrs Harvey-Kelly at Castle Brae, Chesterton, Cambridge and would be grateful if you would reply there.

Yours sincerely,
H. Rochester Sneath
Headmaster

Wimbledon College
Edge Hill
SW 19

May 1st, 1948

Dear Sir,

Your letter has been passed on to me by the Rector of Beaumont College, who is indisposed and unfit for violent exertions. I quite understand the predicament in which you find yourself, and will make a point of coming down to Selhurst School, if you will let me know the date of your return from Chesterton.

It will be necessary for you to have ready for me the usual Bell, Book and Candle, a gallon of holy water and a packet of salt. The latter is required for sprinkling on a certain part of the ghostly anatomy, so it should be loose and capable of being taken up in pinches.

These operations usually take some time, and remuneration is at the rate of a guinea an hour. An essential condition for success is that all present (myself excepted) should be fasting for at least twenty-four hours before the ceremony begins.

Trusting to hear from you in due course.

Yours sincerely,
John Sinnott,
Headmaster

Rats in the Vestry

To the Headmaster of Oundle

Selhurst School
Near Petworth
Sussex

April 29th, 1948

Dear Headmaster of Oundle,

I am writing to you because I understand from my friend Dr Mortimer Benn that your School has recently been infested with rats, and that you were able to call in a very successful Rodent Operative. It will, perhaps, make things clearer if I explain my position to you. Three weeks ago, during the holidays, I heard from one of the Matrons, that she had discovered a sizeable rat in the Vestry. The good lady being nervous, called in the Fire Brigade, but the animal made good its escape. Subsequently no less than sixty-four rats of various shapes and sizes have been discovered in the precincts of the School with the result that three Matrons have had nervous breakdowns, and the wife of the Chairman of the Board of Governors, who was lunching with me and my wife, had a fit of hysteria upon seeing no less than six of these creatures, and collapsed in a heap, having to be carried away in a blanket. As a result the School will have to reassemble a month late, and at present the operations against the rats are being conducted by the School Chaplain in the form of a shooting expedition, and I understand that after a week's effort they can only claim three victims. Attempts to smoke them out with brown paper proved hardly more successful and in desperation we called in a Jesuit to exorcise them. We are now at our wits' end and would be most grateful if you would let me know as soon as possible the name of your own rat-catcher.

I shall be staying for the next few days with my sister, Mrs Harvey-Kelly at the Castle Brae, Chesterton, Cambridge and would be grateful if you would reply there.

Yours sincerely,
H. Rochester Sneath
Headmaster

The Headmaster
The School
Oundle
Northamptonshire

April 30th, 1948

My dear Headmaster,
   I am very sorry to hear about your rats and don't know that we can really be of very much assistance. However, I have consulted the Bursar, who is responsible for this kind of thing and attach a note from him. It certainly seems to be a very unfair hazard on top of all the other troubles of a Headmaster!
   With all good wishes,

Yours sincerely,
Graham Stainforth

Bursar's Office
13b, Market Place
Oundle
Peterborough

May 1st, 1948

RATS

   We employ a firm called The BRITISH RATIN Co. Limited, Station Place, Letchworth. These people send 'operatives' to the School eight times a year to deal with rats, mice and insects, and there is no doubt that the regular attention obtained in this way does help to keep rats down.
   The Local Authority's Surveyor is supposed to take rats seriously and would conduct a special 'anti-rat' drive if asked to do so.
   Rat poison can of course be obtained from a chemist, but there is always a risk that the rats will die in some inaccessible place and floors may have to be taken up in consequence. Some poisons are said to drive rats into the open. The chemist, or again the Local Authority, will advise.

Bursar.

Mr Robert Agincourt

To the Headmaster of Haileybury

Selhurst School
Near Petworth
Sussex

April 22nd, 1948

Dear Headmaster,

I am writing to you in confidence about a Mr Robert
Agincourt who has applied for the post of Senior French Master
at Selhurst. He informs me that before the war he was for six
years on the Staff at Haileybury, but was unable to furnish me
with any written testimonial from you, since he said that he had
lost it. Naturally the last thing I would want to do would be to
suspect him of any dishonest motives, and indeed I do not doubt
that at Haileybury he proved a model Master and endeared himself
to the Common Room and boys alike. However, it cannot be denied
that his external appearances are all against him, and indeed
boys might well mock at a Master with so prominent a wart upon
his nose, nor, I imagine, could his club foot assist him in refereeing
games. Nevertheless, it may be that beneath this somewhat
distressing exterior, there lurks a capability of inspired teaching,
and an inherent dignity of personality that is belied by his
improbable appearance. If it is not troubling you too far, I should
welcome your views upon Mr Agincourt and you may regard
everything you say as being in the strictest personal confidence.

I shall be spending the next few days with my sister Mrs
Harvey-Kelly at Castle Brae, Chesterton, Cambridge and it would
be most helpful if you would reply there.

Yours sincerely,
H. Rochester Sneath
Headmaster

Haileybury and Imperial Service College
Hertford

April 23rd, 1948

Dear Headmaster,

Thank you for your letter of April 22nd. To the best of my knowledge Mr Robert Agincourt has never been on the staff of Haileybury College, nor can I remember a Master here with a prominent wart upon his nose or a club foot. He is clearly a fraud.

Will you please let me know if you have anything in writing referring to his time at Haileybury. Did you hear of him through an Agency?

Yours sincerely
E. F. Bonhote

P. S. We have a Junior School at Windsor which was the Imperial Service College Junior School. It is just possible that he taught there – but I have no record of it, and in any case it would not be Haileybury.
    The HM is :   E. A. S. M. Beckwith
                  H. & I. S. C. Junior School
                  Clower Manor
                  Windsor

Selhurst School
Near Petworth
Sussex

April 24th, 1948

My dear Canon,

I am writing to thank you very much for your letter. From what you say it is fairly clear that Mr Agincourt could not have taught at Haileybury. On the other hand, he was able to display an intimate knowledge of Haileybury when he produced evidence of an unfortunate scandal, involving the dismissal of two masters, the mysterious death of another and the excommunication of the Chaplain, which allegedly took place during the time that he was a Master there. You will readily understand that it causes me great embarrassment to refer to this topic, which you must have hoped would have been forgotten, and I can assure you that I would not have dreamed of so doing were it not of material assistance in clearing up this mystery. He was not recommended by an agency, but applied to me by letter, having seen my advertisement in *The Times Educational Supplement*.

Yours sincerely,
H. Rochester Sneath
Headmaster

To Sir Adrian Boult

Selhurst School
Near Petworth
Sussex

April 22nd, 1948

Dear Sir Adrian Boult,

As you may perhaps be aware, Selhurst is to hold celebrations for the third centenary of its foundation. Our Musical Tutor, Mr David Price, has composed for the occasion a Symphony that he has dedicated to Selhurst. He is a highly competent musician who received a very long and expensive training under the best Continental Masters, and a Conductor to whom he has shown the score is of the opinion that it is the most significant composition since the war. It is to receive its first hearing, graced I hope by the presence of the Minister of Education, in the middle of June and the Jubilation Committee has unanimously requested me to ask that you will conduct this first performance. I need hardly say how honoured we should be if you were to accede to our request and the first expression of the Selhurst Symphony were to take place under your baton. Mr Price is adamant that a Musician with a name greater than his own should lead the School Orchestra upon so auspicious an occasion.

Yours very truly,
H. Rochester Sneath
Headmaster

The British Broadcasting Corp.
Broadcasting House
London W1

April 28th, 1948

Dear Sir,

Sir Adrian Boult has asked me to thank you very much for your letter of the 22nd and your very kind invitation to him.

Unfortunately he is already extremely booked up in June, and as you do not give him any precise date he is afraid he cannot accept, though he is much touched by your kind thought of him.

He would have liked to have written to you himself, but he is so busy in the Studio at the present time that it is difficult for him to deal with correspondence at this moment.

Yours truly
G. M. Beckett
Secretary to Sir Adrian Boult

To the Headmaster of Ampleforth

Selhurst School
Near Petworth
Sussex

April 22nd, 1948

Dear Headmaster,
   I understand that you have among your boys several who are amateur painters far above the average for their years. I have been requested by a Government Department to organise an exhibition of schoolboy art which is to go to South America for propaganda purposes. We are particularly anxious that such pictures should be typical of the best type of Public School boys – we wish to impress South America with our virility and evidence of a decadent civilisation such as Picasso distortions and youthful impressions of sex will have to be left behind. I am sure that we can reply upon your help in this matter, which is regarded in high Governmental circles as one of considerable importance.
   I am staying for some days with Mrs Harvey-Kelly at Castle Brae, Chesterton, Cambridge, and it would be a great help if you would reply there.

Yours very truly,
H. Rochester Sneath
Headmaster

From The Headmaster
Ampleforth College
York

April 24th, 1948

Dear Headmaster,
   I will hand your letter to one of our Art Masters to see whether we have got anything which would be of interest to you.
   The boys do not return until early next week. If there is something the master concerned will answer you shortly.

Yours sincerely,
V. P. Nevill

After School Certificate, what next?

Ampleforth Abbey
York

April 24th, 1948

Dear Mr Rochester Sneath,

The Headmaster, Fr Paul Nevill, gave me your letter as I am in charge of the art in the school. It interested me very much and I hope that we may be able to help.

You will doubtless want to see the pictures before making up your mind about them. But I ought to say that we hope to exhibit these pictures here on June the 5th, 6th and 7th. Please let me know if this would be likely to clash with your arrangements?

Yours very truly,
Rev Martin Haigh, OSB

Selhurst School
Near Petworth
Sussex

April 29th, 1948

Dear Fr Haigh,

Thank you very much for your letter. It is so good of you to invite me up to Ampleforth to see your pictures when they are exhibited on June 5th, 6th, 7th and I shall look forward to seeing them. I do not know whether the Headmaster would agree to my taking a few forms there as I have done this in many of our leading Schools, in connection with my forthcoming book on Public School education entitled *After School Certificate, What Next?* We can discuss the whole question of the exhibition of Schoolboy Art for South America when we meet, and I may tell you in confidence that the Minister has hopes that we shall produce a really representative selection.

Yours sincerely,
H. Rochester Sneath
Headmaster

To the Headmaster of Harrow

Selhurst School
Near Petworth
Sussex

March 15th, 1948

My dear Headmaster,

I am writing to you on a very painful topic. Last Thursday night, before the School broke up, it came to my notice that two of my boys had missed the Roll-call and evening Prayers. Their Housemaster subsequently discovered that they had got into trouble in London and, upon being questioned, they informed me that this unfortunate occurrence was the result of the bad influence of two Harrovians, who, although not with them at the time, had been at an earlier part of the evening. As they came into contact with the Police I should be most grateful if you would make enquiries about the incident from your end, for my duty to their parents makes it essential that I should guard against the recurrence of so distressing a matter.

I shall be staying with my sister Mrs Harvey-Kelly at Castle Brae, Chesterton, Cambridge for the next two weeks and would be grateful if you would reply here.

Yours sincerely,
H. Rochester Sneath
Headmaster

From The Head Master
Harrow School
Harrow on the Hill

March 16th, 1948

Dear Head Master,

I have received your letter of the 15th March. I am at a loss to know how you would wish me to proceed in the investigation of the allegation which you transmit without the knowledge of further details. If you will send me more information, I will certainly take the matter up in any way it seems possible.

Yours sincerely,
R. W. Moore

Selhurst School
Near Petworth
Sussex

March 18th, 1948

My dear Head Master,

Very many thanks for your prompt reply to my letter. You will appreciate that this is a matter of some delicacy and my boys are naturally unwilling to reveal the names of the two Harrovians concerned. I had thought that your two boys would have been found missing at roll call and my purpose in writing to you was to inform you that they had been in a London night club with two Selhurst boys. My boys were subsequently apprehended by the Police for unruly behaviour but that was after your boys had left them. I thought that you ought to know about this in order that you might guard against it in the future.

Incidentally I have recently been approached by the BBC who are anxious to broadcast a service from our School Chapel in the course of next term. Before making up my mind over this, I should like to have some idea of the practical difficulties involved. I understand that there has been a broadcast of a similar nature from the Harrow School Chapel and I would be most grateful if you could spare me the time to let me know of any practical difficulties that we are likely to encounter. As you are doubtless aware, Selhurst like Harrow has a nationwide reputation for its Unison Singing.

Yours very sincerely,
H. Rochester Sneath
Headmaster

From The Head Master
Harrow School
Harrow on the Hill

March 24th, 1948

Dear Head Master,

Thank you for your further letter of the 18th March. Until you give me fuller information I cannot proceed in this matter. Would you please inform me what are the premises which two Harrovians are alleged to have visited; the time during which it is said that this visit took place; what connection or arrangement, if any, existed between these two boys and the two Selhurst boys; and whether these two boys had had any previous connection with the two Selhurst boys. I should also be glad if any further information could be forthcoming which might enable me to make investigations here. I appreciate that the two Selhurst boys would be reluctant to reveal the names of the other two, but I have no doubt that you obtained all the information which you could before writing to me as you did.

I cannot help you with information about broadcast services. I have always refused to have services in the School Chapel broadcast since I believe that such an arrangement is likely seriously to impair the true value and function of a chapel service.

Yours sincerely,
R. W. Moore

Selhurst School
Near Petworth
Sussex

March 26th, 1948

Dear Head Master,

Thank you for your letter of the 24th March. The only further information which I can give you in this matter is that these boys visited a London night club called the Bagatelle. I understand that your boys left at about 11 pm. My boys inform me that there were no women present. I understand that all the boys had known each other in the holidays. I wrote to you for two reasons. First, I thought that your boys would have been found missing by their Housemasters and you would now know where they had been. And secondly, because even though I realised that you might well be unable to trace the culprits, I owed it to you to let you know that this had taken place. I am sorry that this should be rather unsatisfactory from your point of view, but I hope that perhaps my information may enable you to guard against this sort of thing in the future.

Thank you very much for your comments about broadcast services. That was very much what I felt myself but very strong pressure was brought to bear on me as an old boy now occupies a senior post on the staff of the BBC.

Yours sincerely,
H. Rochester Sneath
Headmaster

From The Head Master
Harrow School
Harrow on the Hill

April 6th, 1948

Dear Head Master,

I fear my reply to your last letter has been held up by pressure of work over the end of term. From what I have been able to find out it seems to me most unlikely that the two boys to whom reference was made were actually members of the school, but I have ascertained that two boys who very recently left the school do frequently go to the Bagatelle for dinner. Incidentally these boys were boys with perfectly good records here and I learn too that the Bagatelle is not a 'night club' but a perfectly respectable restaurant. I think this is probably the most likely explanation. If, on the other hand, your boys concerned are certain that the two others are still or were still at the time *in statu pupillari* then I can only suggest that they be requested to furnish the names on

the understanding – and I am entirely prepared to promise this –
that no punitive action will be taken.

May I thank you again?

Yours sincerely,
R. W. Moore

To the Headmaster of Selhurst School

Blundell's School
Near Tiverton
Devon

March 16th, 1948

Dear Headmaster,

We would be very much privileged if you would care to come and preach a sermon at Blundell's on Sunday May 23rd. You may remember meeting me some years ago at Leatherhead and I also believe that we met once with the Headmaster of Sutton Vallance. If you are able to do this perhaps you would let me know what train you would be likely to catch and I will, of course, arrange for a car to meet you. If you would care to bring your wife, we should be delighted to have you both to stay with us over the weekend. I am very much hoping that we shall see you.

Kind regards,

Yours sincerely,
J. S. Carter
Headmaster

Selhurst School
Near Petworth
Sussex

March 18th, 1948

Dear Sir,

I have been asked by the Headmaster to thank you for your very kind letter and to say that he will be delighted to accept your invitation to preach a sermon at Blundells on Sunday May 23rd. As you will have seen, the school has had to break up owing to a double epidemic and the Headmaster is spending six weeks in Cambridge with his sister Mrs Harvey-Kelly at Castle Brae, Chesterton, Cambridge. He would be grateful if you could let him have further details to that address.

Believe me, I remain,

Yours faithfully,
Dorothy Lord
Private Secretary to the Headmaster

Mrs Harvey Kelly

From The Headmaster
Blundell's School
Tiverton

March 20th, 1948

Dear Miss North,
    I think there is some mistake about the enclosed. Mr Sneath has not been invited to preach at Blundell's.

Yours very truly,
J. S. Carter

Selhurst School
Near Petworth
Sussex

March 27th, 1948

Dear Head Master,
    Thank you for your letter which has been forwarded from the school. The Head Master is at the moment undertaking a lecture tour to the British Forces in Germany. He will be away for about a fortnight.
    However, I am most surprised at your reply to my letter since the Head Master showed me the letter purporting to come from you before he left for Germany. I can only conclude that it must have been some kind of practical joke on the part of someone if, as you say, the invitation did not come from you.
    I will place your letter before the Head Master when he returns and I have no doubt that he will be writing to you then.
    Believe me, I remain,

Yours faithfully,
Dorothy Lord
Private Secretary to the Headmaster

Selhurst School
Near Petworth
Sussex

April 22nd, 1948

Dear Headmaster,

   On my return from Germany my Secretary, Miss Lord,
informed me that you had written to say that the invitation
which I received from you to preach at Blundell's on May 23rd did
not, in point of fact, come from you. I was very surprised to hear
this, and I enclose the letter that I received purporting to come
from you. I think that it must be a practical joke and do not think
that it could be one of my boys.

Yours truly,
H. Rochester Sneath
Headmaster

From The Headmaster
Blundell's School
Tiverton
Devon

April 23rd, 1948

Dear Headmaster,

   Many thanks for your letter together with the practical joke
which I return herewith. Obviously it is no one down here seeing
that the notepaper is not headed and in any case is wrongly
addressed. We are not 'Near Tiverton'. My signature is pretty
bad but not quite so bad as the forger would make out! I can
offer no solution as to the author.

Yours sincerely,
J. S. Carter

Selhurst School
Near Petworth
Sussex

April 24th, 1948

Dear Headmaster,

I have received your letter this morning and I am a little sorry
that you have not taken any steps to discover the author of this
monstrous outrage. I feel I must point out that I have suffered no
little inconvenience as a direct result of your supposed invitation,
for I had subsequently refused an invitation to spend a weekend
with the Archbishop. I had also taken some trouble in the
preparation of a sermon, which was a revised version of one which
I preached with great success at Bonn University. It should be
obvious that anyone connected with your school would be at
pains to make some small error in the heading of the paper in order
to avoid suspicion. I am wondering, therefore, if you have not
too hastily dismissed the matter without making proper enquiries
among your boys. I think that I may fairly claim that you owe
me the courtesy of attempting to solve this matter and if possible,
to rectify it.

Yours sincerely,
H. Rochester Sneath
Headmaster

From The Headmaster
Blundell's School
Tiverton
Devon

April 28th, 1948

Dear Headmaster,

I am sorry that you have been so seriously inconvenienced. I
must confess that I regard it as a silly prank rather than a
monstrous outrage. I did not go into things at this end because we

have no one here from Selhurst. If you wish me to start sleuthing, would you care to return the bogus letter?

Yours sincerely,
J. S. Carter

To the Headmaster of Malvern

Selhurst School
Near Petworth
Sussex

February 25th, 1948

Dear Headmaster,

In view of the slight acquaintance in Birmingham some years ago when we were both members of the same Golf Club, I venture to write to request your support for the nomination of Selhurst for the Headmasters' Conference. I expect that you will recall the somewhat painful circumstances associated with my predecessor which prevented the election of Selhurst to the Headmasters' Conference some fifteen years ago. I now learn unofficially that several prominent Headmasters have agreed to support our nomination when it comes up before the meeting, and your support would contribute materially to the strength of our case. As you are probably aware, Selhurst is a School of 275 boys and we have recently gained our first Open Award at Oxford. My Teaching Staff is composed almost entirely of Oxford and Cambridge Graduates and includes also a Doctor of Philosophy of Munich University and a defeated candidate for Parliament. If you would care to honour the School with a visit you would be most welcome. Unfortunately I have had to close the School down for this term as the result of a double epidemic of chicken pox and German Measles. I am therefore spending a month in Cambridge with my sister Mrs Harvey-Kelly at Castle Brae, Chesterton, Cambridge and would be grateful if you would reply to this address.

Yours sincerely,
H. Rochester Sneath
Headmaster

Headmaster's House
College Road
Tel : Malvern 1472

Malvern College
Headmaster's Office
Main Building
Tel : Malvern 1498

February 28th, 1948

Dear Sneath,

Thank you very much for your letter of February 25th. I would gladly do what was possible to assist, but in point of fact your nomination to the Headmasters' Conference will go before the Committee of which I am not a member.

Incidentally, it is important to remember that it is not the School, but the individual Headmaster who is actually elected as a member of the Conference.

Many thanks for your letter and memories.

With all good wishes,

Yours sincerely,
H. C. A. Gaunt

c/o Mrs Harvey-Kelly
Castle Brae
Chesterton
Cambridge

March 15th, 1948

My dear Gaunt,

Please forgive my very long delay in replying to your very kind letter, but as you may possibly remember, I am a lay-preacher and have been travelling around the countryside. It is good of you to offer to assist our election to the Headmasters' Conference and I understand from two friends of mine who are on the Committee that the election is a foregone conclusion.

I do not know whether I can persuade you to preach the sermon at our Speech Weekend on Sunday June 20th. Mr

A Doctor of Philosophy of Munich University

C

Tomlinson, the Minister of Education has kindly agreed to present the prizes on the Saturday. I need hardly say how very glad we shall be to see you.

   With all good wishes to you and your wife,

Yours sincerely,
H. Rochester Sneath
Headmaster

Headmaster's House	Malvern College
College Road	Headmaster's Office
Tel : Malvern 1472	Main Building
	Tel : Malvern 1498

March 18th, 1948

Dear Sneath,
   Thank you very much for your letter of March 15th but I am awfully sorry that I can't come on Sunday, June 20th and all weekends for next term are booked.

Yours sincerely,
H. C. A. Gaunt

To the Headmaster of Selhurst School

18 Canonbury Square
London, N1

March 19th, 1948

Dear Dr Sneath,

I was discussing with my friend Dr Gaunt, the Headmaster of Malvern last week the possibilities of another public school for my younger son Oswald, aged ten years, and he happened to mention the name of Selhurst. My elder son Christopher was at Malvern, is quite emphatic that Malvern would not suit Oswald at all and I am inclined to agree with him.

Although I confess that I have not heard of Selhurst I am anxious to try something quite new as my late husband, Brigadier Jack Worsley was nothing if not modern in his ideas.

Perhaps you would be good enough to give me some details of Selhurst and its varied activities. Oswald is a sensitive child and not unintelligent, although he is very fond of school debating and I have no doubt that you will be able to provide any special treatment which may be desirable for him.

Perhaps I have not made it quite clear that I am anxious for Oswald's name to be put on your waiting list.

Yours sincerely,
Henrietta Worsley

Selhurst School
Near Petworth
Sussex

My dear Mrs Worsley,

I thank you very much for your letter. I am indeed glad that my dear friend Mr H. C. A. Gaunt has mentioned my name to you and that of our illustrious school. I would be delighted to do all that I can for you. I must, however, point out that a school of our standing has few if any vacancies at the best of times and at the moment we have a waiting list which is full until 1962 and I have many tentative offers until 1965. However, the best course for you to adopt is for you to write to the Domestic Bursar, the Reverend

Wotan Sneath, sending him a registration fee of £8 which is non-recoverable and your son's name will be placed upon our waiting list for the Waiting List.

I am interested though not entirely surprised to hear that you think that Malvern is unsuitable for your second boy. The day of the conventional public school is now over. At Selhurst we endeavour, and I think with some success, to provide a truer and nobler concept of education. My staff is recruited from a very wide cross section of talent and includes a Doctor of Philosophy from Munich and a man, Mr Digby Groat, who recently forfeited his deposit in a by-election where he was standing as a King's Cavalier. My brother, the Rev Wotan Sneath, the School Chaplain has had a career of unusual distinction. He was considered for a fellowship of his college and then was received into the orders of the Roman Catholic Church where he reached the dignity of a minor prelate. Troubled by intellectual doubts he left the Roman fold and became a Congregationalist Minister and in 1929 was Moderator of the Free Church Council. Believing that the unity of the Christian Churches was essential he subsequently took Anglican orders and his promotion has been so rapid that he is now on nodding terms with a Colonial Bishop and numbers among his friends a rural dean and a Canon of the Church of Ireland. He is, as you will appreciate, fully qualified to minister to boys of no less than three religious persuasions.

Should we have a vacancy for your boy he will find Selhurst a vigorous and expanding School. We now have 275 boys and our School clubs include a Communist Club and an affiliated branch of the Housewives League. You will therefore see that he will have ample opportunity for debate.

Dear Lady, it was delightful to hear from you and I am wondering whether your late husband was the 'Foxy' Worsley that I used to know many years ago. I could tell you a few things about him!

Yours very sincerely,
H. Rochester Sneath
Headmaster

To the Headmaster of St Benedict's, Ealing

Selhurst School
Near Petworth
Sussex

March 30th, 1948

Dear Headmaster,

I am writing to you upon a most delicate topic. It has been brought to my notice that some days before the end of term, two of my boys broke bounds, missed Evening Prayers and went off to London. Upon questioning they affirmed that it was under the influence of two of your boys who had, however, left them by the time the trouble started. As it involves, or may perhaps involve, Police action, I should be grateful if you would take steps to ensure that there is no recurrence of such an unfortunate event.

I shall be passing the holidays in Ireland and would be grateful if you would reply to me at Ballyfree, Glenealy, Co. Wicklow.

Yours sincerely,
H. Rochester Sneath
Headmaster

From The Head Master
St Benedict's School
Ealing
W5

April 9th, 1948

Dear Headmaster,

I received your most extraordinary communication only on Tuesday last, as your letter was delivered originally to the Ealing County Grammar School, whence it was apparently returned to you. The postscript, however, is unsigned and as the letter is not specifically addressed to me, I do not feel under any obligation whatsoever to reply to your communication.

You may also be unaware that this School is entirely a day school and that I take no responsibility whatsoever for the actions of our boys except in School hours. If you have any complaints to make, you should make them to the parents of the boys concerned. I therefore propose to take no steps whatsoever until I have been furnished with complete information about the incident you refer to. I shall then decide, without prejudice, whether I shall take any action or not.

Yours sincerely,
J. B. Orchard

To the Headmaster of Tonbridge

Selhurst School
Near Petworth
Sussex

March 30th, 1948

Dear Rootie,

You will doubtless remember old 'Tubby' Sneath – well it will
give you a helluva shock, you old bounder, because last year I
took on the Headship here. Do you remember prophesying my
early death in a South American brothel? I must say that I never
imagined that you would get muddled up in this racket either, and
imagine my surprise when I returned from India to be told that
the man whom I had carried home, drunk as a coot seven times a
week, should have got a job. At least I presume the Headmaster
of Tonbridge is you!

Listen Rootie, quite seriously, Selhurst is having a beano for its
three hundredth anniversary on June 19th. Could you come down,
old boy, and give us a sermon on the Sunday? I've got the bleeding
Minister, Tomlinson I mean, coming down on the Saturday to dole
out the pots. Mind you behave yourself and don't start making
eyes at the Matron, even though she may remind you of Vera
Grant.

Let me know, old boy, and give Phyllis and the kids a kiss
from me and please reply to me c/o R. L. Bidwell, Ballyfree
House, Glenealy, Co. Wicklow, as I am staying in Ireland for a
month.

All the best you old swab and have one on me.

Tubby

The Headmaster
The School House
Tonbridge, Kent

March 31st, 1948

Dear Sir,

I have received from you a letter opening 'Dear Rootie'. It is
not intended for me though addressed to the Headmaster of

Tonbridge. In view of the contents of the letter I should be obliged if you would send me the name of the person to whom you have written as Headmaster of Tonbridge and on what the incorrect information is based; for if it is widely presumed that he is Headmaster of Tonbridge that needs correcting for reasons obvious to you.

I am going away on Saturday and my address will be :

LONG CLOSE

LYDDINGTON, NR SWINDON, WILTS

Yours faithfully,
E. E. A. Whitworth

To the Headmaster of Eton

Selhurst School
Near Petworth
Sussex

April 22nd, 1948

My dear Headmaster of Eton,

I am reliably informed that you are to retire from the Headmastership of Eton next July, and I would be more than grateful if you would inform me how I might get my name placed upon the list of candidates to succeed you. I am, as you see, an MA and my age is forty-seven. At the time of my appointment to Selhurst twenty years ago, I was the youngest Headmaster of any of the leading Schools in the country. Previous to that I had spent five years as Senior Languages Master at a leading Public School in South America and I have many unsolicited testimonials from some of the most distinguished and aristocratic inhabitants of that Continent which I could send you by registered post. During my Headmastership of Selhurst we achieved our first connection with Debrett, in that I was instrumental in obtaining as a pupil the nephew of a Life Baron. We have steadily progressed and Selhurst parents now include a Count of the Holy Roman Empire and a Knight Bachelor's divorcee. I have been considered as a Parliamentary candidate and represented the Schools of Britain upon the Milk Marketing Board. My connections with the aristocracy are many, and indeed my wife was for many years the governess of the children of a baronet of ancient lineage. During my Headmastership the number of boys at Selhurst has risen from 49 to 275. I am not yet a member of the Headmaster's Conference, although I understand that my election is to come before the next meeting of the Committee, so that having obtained the recognition of Selhurst as one of the leading Schools of the country, I should then be free to take up an appointment at Eton. I am prepared to submit myself to the approbation of the Governors, and I think that I can say without fear of contradiction, that were I to be chosen Eton would have as its Headmaster a man whose scholastic career has already proved one of distinction and who would bring to his task powers of organisation that the Chairman of my Board of Governors has described as outstanding.

Sir, I await your kind consideration and that of your Governors.

Yours sincerely,
H. Rochester Sneath
Headmaster

To the Manager of the Albert Hall

Selhurst School
Near Petworth
Sussex

April 22nd, 1948

Dear Sir,

It has been decided to hold a monster rally of Old Selhurstians in connection with the coming celebration of the third centenary of the foundation of the school. So many applications have come in that the Jubilation Committee has had to abandon its original intention of hiring the parish hall for the occasion and to search for something more spacious. I should therefore be obliged if you would send me particulars of the formalities necessary for the hiring of the Albert Hall and of the approximate cost of one night. Would there be any hour by which the celebrations would have to end and is there any ban on the provision of alcoholic liquors? I suppose that there are arrangements to prevent any noise occurring inside from reaching the street as we do not wish to incommode the neighbours.

I shall be staying with Mrs Harvey-Kelly at Castle Brae, Chesterton, Cambridge, for some days and would be grateful if you would reply there.

Yours truly,
H. Rochester Sneath
Headmaster

Royal Albert Hall
Kensington Gore
London SW 7

April 26th, 1948

Dear Sir,

I have your letter of the 22nd of April concerning a possible rally of Old Selhurstians. Since you do not say when this is to held, there is little I can tell you about dates, except that the Hall is fully let for the latter half of this year and almost so for the first half of next year.

The Hall is licensed and has its own catering department, and it is rare for anything that takes place in the Hall to be more than barely audible outside.

You give me no idea of the numbers to be accommodated but I think you would probably find this Hall rather big for your purpose since here you would have accommodation for up to about 5,000 people.

The rent of the Hall for an evening for a concert or similar function with a seated audience would be £187 10s 0d but this amount would be substantially increased if you were contemplating a dance and required a dance floor laid in the arena.

Yours faithfully,
C. S. Taylor
Manager

To the Warden of Radley

April 23rd, 1948

Dear Headmaster,

As you are doubtless aware, there is a vacancy for a new Schools match at Lords next year. I am unofficially informed by a leading member of the MCC that the choice lies between our two Schools and that opinion is almost evenly divided. I have no hesitation in saying that although Selhurst has always refused to join the Headmasters' Conference despite repeated pressing, we should not refuse the honour of a match at Lords. The Committee are balancing, I am informed, the greater numbers and the personal reputation of I. P. Campbell against the greater age and tradition of Selhurst and its numerous old boys, prominent in every walk of life. We are helped, also, by the fact that most of the outstanding cricketers at the beginning of the Century have played on the School ground in Sussex County Matches, and no less than three Sussex Captains have been Old Boys. We have also engaged a prominent Test Player as our coach for this season, and five peers have promised to be present at the Selhurst dinner a few days before the decision is to be made. I think it likely, therefore, that we might well be invited to play our principal fixture there next year. However, I realise that this might well cause you some disappointment so I am writing to propose that we should arrange an annual fixture. There is little doubt that this happy compromise would prove most acceptable to the MCC which is at present strongly divided upon the issue, and that we should be invited to hold this fixture at the Headquarters of Cricket. I should be grateful to hear soon if you would prefer to accept this solution or whether you would rather continue to compete for the fixture. I do not know which is your chief match of the season – I understand that it is against some Secondary School – but I would point out that the honour of Lords match is very great and should not be permitted to any that cannot justly be termed Leading Public Schools.

I shall be staying for some days with my sister, Mrs Harvey-Kelly at Castle Brae, Chesterton, Cambridge and would be grateful if you would reply there.

Yours sincerely,
H. Rochester Sneath

To the Headmaster of Winchester

Selhurst School
Near Petworth
Sussex

March 15th, 1948

My dear Oakeshott,
    As you are no doubt aware Selhurst is to celebrate the three
hundredth anniversary of its foundation on June 20th. It was
founded by the Puritan leader Ebenezer Okeshot, who I understand
was one of your distinguished ancestors. We would therefore
regard it as a signal honour if you would come down on the day
that I have named to unveil a plaque to your forebear. This day
has been set aside for our Speech Day and the Minister of
Education has agreed to come and present the prizes. The plaque
is a simple portrait of our Founder above it is his family motto
'Let the Oak Shoot' and below it the School motto 'From an Acorn
to an Oak Tree'.
    Owing to an epidemic the School has broken up early and I am
staying with my sister, Mrs Harvey-Kelly at Castle Brae,
Chesterton, Cambridge and would be obliged if you would address
your reply there.

Yours sincerely,
H. Rochester Sneath
Headmaster

From the Secretary to the Headmaster, Winchester College
The College
Winchester

March 16th, 1948

Dear Sir,
    In the absence of the Headmaster, who has recently departed
by air for Salt Lake City, I am answering your letter of March
15th. The Headmaster would, I know, wish me to express his
regret at missing such a ceremony. Before he left, I understood him
to say that he was to visit Ebenezer Okeshot's grave in Utah, where
as you will doubtless recall the great man breathed his last, after

that quarrel with the Pilgrim Mothers fraught with such momentous consequences for the history of the Middle West. Incidentally I have always understood that since the introduction of the breech-loading gun, the family have preferred the Greek version of the motto, as being less liable to misunderstanding. Doubtless, however, the School authorities have good reason for retaining the older form of it.

According to present plans, the Headmaster will be away for about a year. But I will certainly submit your letter to him. Meanwhile may I on his behalf express the hope that the epidemic to which reference is made in your letter may not prove to be too serious?

I have the honour to be, Sir,

Your obedient servant,
Angela Thacklethwycke
(Private Secretary)

Ebenezer Okeshot

The Daily Worker, April 13th, 1948

A Language Ban

Although I am not a member of the Communist Party, I would like to draw attention to a matter which is not generally known.

I am endeavouring to institute the compulsory study of Russian in this school but have met with every form of obstruction.

The majority of parents have raised quite unreasonable objections and the examination authorities will not set papers in the subject.

The Board of Trade will not issue permits for the import of Russian textbooks, and it is almost impossible to obtain them secondhand.

English is taught in every Russian school; ought we not to grasp this hand of friendship?

H. Rochester Sneath
Headmaster, Selhurst School, Petworth,
Sussex

To the Headmaster of Selhurst School

256, Edge Lane Drive
Liverpool 14

April 13th, 1948

Dear Sir,

I have just read your letter in today's paper and am taking the liberty of sending you a cutting from the *Daily Express* which you may not have seen. It would be interesting to know why and when, if at all, the order by the Board of Education was countermanded.

I have made a copy of the cutting so you need not return it.

I was very pleased to see your protest.

Yours sincerely,
(*Mrs*) *Emma L. Harkness*

The Daily Worker, May 3rd, 1948

Textbooks

On April 13 you printed a letter from a correspondent who stated that the Board of Trade refused to allow the import of Russian textbooks. This is incorrect.

The import of textbooks in a foreign language from the country of origin (ie, textbooks in Russian being supplied from the US) would only be licensed as part of the quota of learned, scientific and technical books allowed to be imported from the US. The permitted amount, as in the case of imports of textbooks from other countries, is 200 per cent of the value of pre-war imports from that country.

M. Balfour
Chief Information Officer,
Board of Trade,
London, SW 1

'You speak Russian, no?'

To the Headmaster of Selhurst School

UNIVERSITY OF LONDON
SCHOOL OF SLAVONIC AND EAST EUROPEAN STUDIES
London WC 1

April 14th, 1948

Dear Sir,

I hope you will not mind my saying that I think your letter
to *The Daily Worker* does a disservice to the cause which you are
trying to espouse. In the first place, why should you suppose that
the compulsory teaching of Russian in present circumstances
would meet with general approval? Why not accept the world
in which you live and try to introduce the subject among those
pupils who are anxious and willing to learn voluntarily for a
start? In the second place, why worry about text-books from the
USSR when there are quite a lot of not-too-awful English textbooks available? And also, why worry the Board of Trade for
licences when there is Collet's Russian Bookshop (67 Great
Russell St WC 1) with its licence to import books from the USSR?
And finally, what is the examination authority that will not
provide examinations in Russian? London does, the Northern Joint
Board does, and I think Oxford and Cambridge does. Then there
are Royal Society of Arts examinations, as well as the University
of London Certificate of Proficiency. In 1947 two pupils sat for
Russian at the General Schools examinations in the whole
country, and this would suggest that there are more
examinations available than students requiring them. What
is more, there is only a handful of teachers in the country
competent to teach Russian, so what would be the good of
trying to introduce it widely in the school at present?
What is needed is a long and necessarily slow process of
co-operation between schools and universities to produce
teachers who can introduce the subject in schools, and that
work is already going on here and in other universities. Our
experience seems to indicate that wherever a teacher has the
knowledge of the language and sufficient confidence to teach it,
a school will introduce the subject – but slowly at first and only

for a few years, and the best service we can render is to be optimistic about our work and not make things seem more difficult than they are.

Yours faithfully,
Dorothy Dalton
Secretary

To the Headmaster of Selhurst School

UNIVERSITY OF LONDON
SCHOOL OF SLAVONIC AND EAST EUROPEAN STUDIES
London WC 1

STUDENTS' UNION SOCIETY

April 15th, 1948

Dear Sir,

We read with considerable interest your letter in the *Daily Worker* in connection with your experiences concerning the teaching of Russian in your school.

I enclose an information statement issued by the Students' Union here on this subject, and a more detailed account of your experiences would be of extreme value to us! We were particularly interested in your reference to the examination authorities, and the question of textbooks. We have found no difficulty here with obtaining textbooks, although those we use are not fully satisfactory. Have you been in touch with Collett's Russian Dept. in connection with Soviet textbooks : they had a supply of elementary Russian grammars from the Soviet Union a couple of months ago!

Any further information you can give us, or suggestions and comments on our statement, will be very welcome.

Yours faithfully,
R. W. Davies
President

To the Headmaster of Selhurst School

NEWS REVIEW
The British Newsmagazine

Editorial Department
185 to 192, High Holborn, London, WC1

April 13th, 1948

VP/GA

Dear Mr Sneath,

I am interested in your letter in today's *Daily Worker*, and would be obliged if you could ring me tomorrow (Wednesday) so that I can fix an appointment to interview you in connection with the difficulty of teaching Russian.

Yours faithfully,
V. Prager

To Mr V. Prager of *News Review*

Selhurst School
Near Petworth
Sussex

April 19th, 1948

Dear Mr Prager,
   The Headmaster has directed me to thank you for your letter
of the 13th inst. and to apologise for his delay in answering it. For
some days he has been seriously ill and this is the first day on which
he has been able to attend to his correspondence. Although he is
now somewhat recovered, the Doctor says that he should not receive
any visitors for some weeks. He is most anxious, however, to
assist you, and, since the School has not yet reassembled, it would
be fruitless for you to go down there. He suggests, therefore that
you send him a list of questions that he will answer to the best
of his ability. He would prefer this method, for he is desirous that
any views publicly expressed should be his own rather than those of
his subordinates, and he is convinced that he would be able to
supply information sufficient for your purposes. He is of the opinion
that your interest is a public service, and he hopes that it will not
be prevented by his unfortunate inability to grant an interview.
In conclusion he says that he would not insist upon a literal
transcription of his words, for having taken your paper for some
years, he recognises that one of its finest characteristics is its modern
and vigorous English style.
   He was taken ill while visiting his sister Mrs Harvey-Kelly at
Castle Brae, Chesterton, Cambridge, and, since it has not been
possible to move him, it would save time if you would address
your reply there.

Yours truly,
Penelope Pox-Rhyddene
Secretary

To the Headmaster of Selhurst School

TELEGRAM

April 13th

KINGSCROSS REDIRECTED FROM PETWORTH

SNEATH C/O MRS HARVEY KELLY CASTLE BRAE CHESTERTON
CAMBRIDGE

PLEASE RING PRAGER OF NEWS REVIEW TEMPLE BAR 246 EXTENSION
848 WEDNESDAY MORNING = PRAGER

News Review, April 22nd, 1948

WHO IS ROCHESTER SNEATH?

It was an intriguing – a most intriguing letter. The signature over which it appeared last week in the *Daily Worker*'s correspondence columns was 'H. Rochester Sneath'.

Mr Sneath was described as 'Headmaster of Selhurst School, Petworth, Sussex' which made his letter even more interesting, for in it the Headmaster said this :

> Although I do not happen to be a member of your Communist Party . . . I am endeavouring to institute the comulsory* study of Russian in this School, but have been met with every form of obstruction. The majority of the parents have raised quite unreasonable objections, and the Examination Authorities will not set papers in the subject. The Board of Trade will not issue permits for the importation of Russian text-books.
>
> . . . As one who has spent many years in Russia, and grown to love and admire the Russian people, I am convinced that the only means of a true friendship is for the youth of each country to learn the other's language. English is taught in every Russian school : ought we not to grasp this hand of friendship?

News Review's first thought, on reading this epistle, was to find and quiz the friendly headmaster, and it was then the question 'Who is Rochester Sneath'? first formed in the reporter's mind.

For the telephone service failed to find him; Directory Enquiry could not help. The Post Office did not know the school's precise location. Petworth's police were baffled.

The National Union of Teachers could furnish no information, nor could the scholastic agencies.

Vexed and mystified, *News Review* posted a letter and sent a telegram to Mr H. R. Sneath, of Selhurst School, near Petworth, but no answer had arrived by the time this page went to press.

A search through the *Daily Worker*'s files yielded Mr Sneath's original letter. It was typed on printed letter-heading, gave the school's telephone number as Petworth 56. Oddest thing of all was that Sheila Lynd, the *Worker*'s Feature Editor, had written to the

* Presumably a typist's error

Headmaster's address asking permission to publish his letter, and had received a reply.

This, signed by Mr Sneath's secretary Dorothy Lord, gave the permission sought, and explained that the Headmaster 'is in Germany for the next fortnight lecturing to the British Forces.'

There could thus be no question of a misprint in the *Daily Worker*'s published version of Headmaster Sneath's address. Yet when *News Review* called Petworth 56 on the telephone it was to discover that no such number existed, for the simple reason that some time ago Petworth Exchange went over to four figures.

MYSTERY DEEPENS

Petworth itself, *News Review*'s inquiring reporter discovered, is a picturesque old village of 2362 inhabitants huddled round the walls of Petworth House, Sussex seat of Charles Henry Wyndham, third Baron Leconfield. There the mystery deepened. The local estate agency had no Rochester Sneath on its books; the local school-master did not recall the name; nor did the secretary of Seaford College, evacuated to Petworth since the beginning of the war.

All the 'regular channels' – the village solicitors, the receptionist at Petworth's Swan Hotel, the barman, the 'old customers' at the inns – were questioned in vain.

At last one slender thread of information was obtained. Mr Rochester Sneath had written to the local Post Office asking that any letters which might arrive should be forwarded. Quite rightly the forwarding address was not disclosed to *News Review*.

Then another small fact was elicited from the postal authorities : *News Review*'s letter and telegram to Mr Sneath had gone through.

Shifting its inquiry, *News Review* tried Selhurst Park Farm, not far from Portsmouth. No Mr Sneath was known. A Mr W. C. Sneath, living in Hove said he was 'no relation'.

Fourteen universities in England, Scotland and Wales, among them the Universities of London, Oxford, Cambridge, Manchester and Birmingham had no record on their graduates' registers of Mr Sneath, whose printed letter-heading described him as an MA and a L-es-L.* This suggested that he took his degree elsewhere.

Finally, the War Office, the RAF, the Control Commission for Germany and the British Council could not remember engaging any Rochester Sneath, Headmaster of Selhurst School, to lecture to the Forces in Germany.

An exhausted reporter hopes Mr Sneath will spot this article. If so, *News Review* would appreciate a call. Headmasters who want to teach their pupils Russian are so rare.

* Licencié-es-Lettres is a French degree: Bachelor of Arts, First Class.

H.Rochester Sneath, M.A., L-es-L.,

H. Rochester Sneath, MA, L-es-L, passes on

After I had replied to Mr Prager's letter of April 13th, 1948 and his telegram on April 19th I found a reporter from *News Review* on the doorstep of my friend's lodgings.

News Review carried an article on April 29th entitled 'Death of Rochester Sneath' in which it was made inferentially clear that I was the culprit. A cascade of any Headmagisterial letters descended on Sir Montagu Butler, the father of R. A. Butler, the Master of Pembroke College. He formally rebuked me and pronounced his sentence. I think that I saw a twinkle in his eye for he had showed me great kindness as a junior undergraduate, and our relationship was happy and unchanged when, in 1950, I was showed into the College after my two year exile.